A CENTURY *of*
BOURNEMOUTH

Russell-Cotes Art Gallery and Museum, 2001. Used for many years as a painting store, Gallery Four has been returned to its original décor and opened once again as an art gallery, displaying works by women artists from the collection, many purchased by Merton Russell-Cotes. *(Russell-Cotes Art Gallery and Museum Collection/James Howe)*

A CENTURY *of* BOURNEMOUTH

LOUISE PERRIN

IT IS NO
CRIME
TO KISS, IN
BOURNEMOUTH.

"To Err is human, to kiss, divine"

First published in the United Kingdom in 2002 by
Sutton Publishing Limited exclusively for
WHSmith, Greenbridge Road, Swindon SN3 3LD

British Library Cataloguing in Publication Data
A catalogue record for this book is available from the British Library.

ISBN 0-7509-3119-1

Illustrations

Front endpaper: Beales' Christmas celebrations, *c.* 1912. (*Courtesy of Beales' Archive*)
Back endpaper: Bournemouth Symphonic Brass, 2002. (*Russell-Cotes Art Gallery and Museum Collection*)
Half title page: An unusual view of the lower end of Bath Hill, 1920s. The baths, built by Roberts & Co. in 1888, are still here, but the sign on the left refers to Jones & Seward who were awarded the contract for clearing the land and laying the foundations for the new Pavilion. An advert for the baths in 1888 offered to transport sea water to any part of town. (*Russell-Cotes Art Gallery and Museum Collection*)
Title page: A cheeky postcard from about 1910 addressed to a young woman in Totton. Due to its distance from London, Bournemouth never developed the reputation of Brighton as a place for clandestine rendezvous. (*Russell-Cotes Art Gallery and Museum Collection*)

Typeset in 11/14pt Photina and produced by
Sutton Publishing Limited, Phoenix Mill,
Thrupp, Stroud, Gloucestershire GL5 2BU.
Printed and bound in England by
J.H. Haynes & Co. Ltd, Sparkford.

Russell-Cotes Art Gallery and Museum
East Cliff
Bournemouth
BH1 3AA
Tel 01202 451 800 (recorded message)

www.russell-cotes.bournemouth.gov.uk

The Russell-Cotes Art Gallery and Museum (306288) and the Joseph Lucas Collection (237475) are Charities registered with the Charity Commissioners and administered by Bournemouth Borough Council.

BOURNEMOUTH BOROUGH COUNCIL
Leisure & Tourism Directorate
Arts, Library & Museum Services

Contents

Aerial view of the East Cliff, taken between 1951 and 1955. *(Russell-Cotes Art Gallery and Museum Collection)*

Introduction

Bournemouth, uniquely among English seaside resorts, did not develop around an existing fishing village or centre of population. People have lived in the area we now call Bournemouth since prehistoric times. Archaeological evidence and early maps show scattered settlements, isolated houses and farms across the heathland and at strategic river crossings. The modern town of Bournemouth grew as a direct consequence of people wishing to visit for the purpose of sea-bathing, beginning with Lewis Tregonwell, the 'Father of Bournemouth'. In 1810 he purchased 8½ acres of land from Sir George Tapps on which he built a summer residence for himself and his family; the house is now part of the Exeter Hotel. This first seaside home in Bournemouth was also let to friends and Tregonwell later purchased additional plots totalling 63 acres on which he built further houses for letting during the summer season.

Sir George William Tapps-Gervis, who became Lord of the Manor of Christchurch following the death of his father in 1835, saw the potential of the area to become an exclusive watering place. The fashion for sea-bathing had emerged at the end of the eighteenth century and where many people had previously travelled to Bath or Buxton to 'take the cure', they now began to visit the spas that were springing up along the coast. Sir George owned land along the seafront and eastwards towards modern day Boscombe, and began to develop that part of his estate to the east of the Bourne River. He built elegant villas along what was to become Westover Road, leading to the Bath Hotel. By 1838 Bournemouth's history as a uniquely visitor-led town had begun.

FROM WATERING PLACE TO SEASIDE RESORT

In 1901 Bournemouth was a sizeable and prosperous seaside town with a reputation as one of England's major coastal resorts. In less than eighty years the town had experienced a phenomenal increase in population from 695 inhabitants in 1851 to 154,677 by 1891. Bournemouth became a district under the 1856 Improvement Act, governed by a Board of Commissioners and covering an area of 1-mile radius from the front door of the Belle Vue Hotel (where the Pavilion is now). The town achieved municipal borough status in 1890, with a governing body of eighteen councillors who had the authority to appoint a mayor and responsibility for an area of 2,660 acres. Furthermore, the town, which had an indirect and inconvenient rail link to London via Ringwood from 1870, finally gained a direct line to London via Brockenhurst terminating at the new Bournemouth East station in 1886. The station was renamed Bournemouth Central in 1899. The town's lovely coastline was now less than 2½ hours away from London.

But the town's governing body could not afford to become complacent. Competition for visitors and the income they brought was fierce between south coast resort rivals such as

Brighton and Eastbourne. Bournemouth could either continue to cater for its mainly affluent clientele, with an emphasis on invalids and the elderly, or promote itself as a fashionable resort, along the lines of the French Riviera made popular by the visits of Queen Victoria in the last twenty years of her life.

Attitudes to the seaside were changing. The nineteenth century had promoted seaside visiting as the virtuous cleansing of mind and body; the twentieth century was to see the development of the notion of rest, relaxation and the family. Health was evolving into holiday. Many more people had the opportunity to take a holiday, and workers had been entitled to Bank Holidays since an Act of 1871. Easter Monday, Whit Monday and the August Bank Holiday were hugely popular for a trip to the sea by train. Even so, an advert from the visitors' guide to the Royal Bath Hotel as late as 1910 continued to point out the benefits of Bournemouth as a place where the visitor was less likely to die from an infection compared with other resorts.

"Of the leading English health resorts, those with the next best records Bournemouth are :—

ZYMOTIC DEATH-RATES.

	1894	1895	1896	1897	1898	Average.
Eastbourne	0·54	0·99	1·04	0·86	1·26	0·93
Hastings	0·98	1·03	1·16	0·78	1·27	1·04
Cheltenham	0·77	0·96	1·72	1·30	0·85	1·12
Bath	2·14	0·62	0·92	1·02	0·95	1·13
Southport	1·14	0·91	1·15	1·19	1·51	1·18
Dover	0·35	1·53	2·65	1·47	2·29	1·65
Brighton	1·21	1·75	1·63	1·64	2·36	1·71

There were bitter arguments between the varying factions, residents and visitors, shopkeepers and hoteliers, and the political affiliations of those who governed, all with different visions of the future. Older residents wanted things to stay 'as they were' while people with commercial interests saw change as essential to progress and prosperity. The columns and letter pages of local newspapers were often the battleground.

Arguments over the decision to build the Pavilion lasted for nearly thirty years, although the intervention of the First World War added to the delay. An entertainment venue with a concert room, theatre, dance hall and cafés had been part of the Borough's plans since 1890. Various schemes were proposed and suggestions made about the most appropriate site. In 1909 people who objected to the Pavilion being licensed premises successfully opposed one scheme and there were several public inquiries. After the First World War a new scheme was drafted and the council finally approved it, although not without further public consultation about how much it would cost. The Duke of Gloucester finally opened the new Pavilion in 1929.

There were also contradictory opinions about the building of the Undercliff Drive to the east of the pier, supporters seeing it as essential both for the control of cliff erosion and as a facility for the town. The dissenters felt it would change the essential character of the town, increasing development along the shore, and questioned the motives of supporters, some of whom it was felt had financial interests vested in the scheme.

But by 1910 Bournemouth had an extension to the Pier, the Undercliff Drive was built, and plans were approved for extending it further east and west towards Alum Chine. Mr and Mrs Russell-Cotes (later to become Sir Merton and Lady Russell-Cotes) had built their seaside villa on the east cliff; they filled it with wonderful curios and souvenirs from their travels around the world, and with works of art. The couple later donated the house and its contents to the people of Bournemouth to become the town's art gallery and museum. By 1910 there were also plans to build a brand new swimming pool and baths to replace the old Victorian ones. Even the original 1838 villas along Westover Road were slowly being turned into commercial premises, and the whole row had disappeared by 1931 to become one of the town's major commercial streets.

A CHANGING TOWN

The local authority became a county borough in 1901, establishing schools and libraries, and developing the infrastructure required of a modern town. The town grew far beyond the 1-mile radius of the Belle Vue Hotel and encompassed neighbouring villages and

Portman Building, Richmond Hill, 2002. *(Russell-Cotes Art Gallery and Museum Collection/Martin Coyne)*

Bournemouth Library, 2002. *(Russell-Cotes Art Gallery and Museum Collection/Martin Coyne)*

settlements, such as Kinson, Iford, Holdenhurst and Throop, some of which were not subsumed willingly. Bournemouth had many boundary changes in the twentieth century, perhaps the most dramatic being the relocation from Hampshire into Dorset in 1974. On 1 April 1997 the town became a unitary authority, and the organisation of local government changed from a committee to a cabinet-style structure in 2002.

Bournemouth has always been prepared to meet the changing demands of the latest wave of visitors. This can be seen clearly in the sequence of development along the seafront and particularly around Pier Approach. No one could have anticipated today's levels of traffic in 1900 when the council had a Horse and Hackney Carriage Committee and cars had only just begun to appear on the town's roads. The provision of indoor bathing and swimming facilities on the seafront has been a feature of the town since its earliest days. Swimming facilities were later moved to the Leisure Pool at the Bournemouth International Centre, although this may not continue further into the twenty-first century as development plans for the BIC may include the replacement of the pool by additional conference facilities. Needless to say, this is causing heated debate in local circles.

Bournemouth, although a holiday resort, has not existed in isolation from the outside world. With the rest of the United Kingdom it began the twentieth century as part of an empire; today it is part of a worldwide global economy. The world events of the twentieth

View from the Bournemouth Eye, 2002. *(Russell-Cotes Art Gallery and Museum Collection/Martin Coyne)*

century have been observed and some have made their mark on the town, not least the two world wars when young men were called up to fight abroad, and those who remained behind fought on the Home Front.

The people of Bournemouth have seen the same social changes as the rest of the country: the development of motor-transport and the aeroplane; improvements in housing; and the arrival of the cinema as mass entertainment, still popular even with the arrival of the video, DVD and home computer. This was a century of changes in communication technology, so much so that the title for this book could be 'From Marconi to Mobile Phones'.

During the 1930s many towns undertook the demolition of inadequate Victorian housing and replaced it with houses that had inside toilets and gardens. Bournemouth experienced much less of this – not being a centre of industry it had few 'slums' to demolish. Similarly in the 1960s, most notably around town centres, many houses and commercial premises were demolished to make way for flyovers and bypasses to improve traffic flow and reduce congested roads. Demographic changes in Bournemouth have reduced the need for large Victorian and Edwardian villas; some have become residential homes, sub-divided into flats, others have been demolished to make way for purpose-built flats.

THE FUTURE?

The century has turned again and Bournemouth is approaching its bicentenary in 2010. Tourism remains the main employer in the area, although the banking, finance and insurance sector is the most valuable to the local economy. Manufacturing accounts for only 6 per cent of the jobs in the authority. The economy has been built on tourism, which is supported by the retail, leisure and entertainment sector in the town, and has diversified into business tourism and the conference market.

Bournemouth has always been rebuilding. From the time when Tregonwell erected his house close to the mouth of the River Bourne there can hardly have been a year without the presence of scaffolding and, latterly, cranes. Debates about the future of the Winter Gardens, revamping the Pavilion, building a surfing reef or marina at Boscombe, or even why the IMAX was built at all, continue. What makes Bournemouth different from every other town in the country is its position on Poole Bay, with miles of glorious sandy beaches, safe clean water, the cliffs that separate town from the beach, acres of gardens and open spaces. We suppose today's visitors to Bournemouth are very different to those of 200 years ago, but are they? *Plus ça change, plus c'est la même chose.* (No superficial or apparent change alters its essential nature.)

Lousie Perrin, 2002

The Dawn of the Twentieth Century

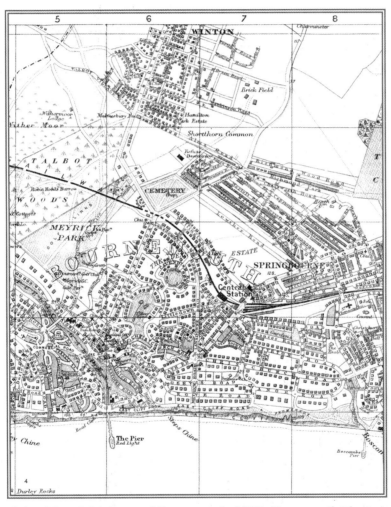

A detail from Bright's map of Bournemouth, 1897. *(Bournemouth Libraries)*

Joseph's Steps, West Cliff, *c.* 1890. The whole of the West Cliff looks rugged and undeveloped. The steps in the picture are where the Zig-Zag is now. At the bottom of the steps the gentlemen's bathing machines were to the right and the ladies' to the left. The sexes were strictly segregated. *(Bournemouth Libraries)*

Bournemouth Pier and Pier Approach, 1900. The entrance to the Pier looks quite splendid, but the surroundings appear almost basic compared to other resorts at the same time. *(Russell-Cotes Art Gallery and Museum Collection)*

Bournemouth Breezes, 1900. This advert is from *Bright's Guide to Bournemouth.* Come to Bournemouth, enjoy the pine-scented air and take some away with you in a bottle – 'Refreshing, Redolent with the odour of pine'. *(Bournemouth Libraries)*

Opening of the Undercliff Drive, 1907. The first section of the Undercliff Drive opened as far as Meyrick Road. The rest was not completed until 1914. This is an unusual view of Sydenham's Reading Room and the baths, clearly visible behind the crowds. *(Bournemouth Libraries)*

Winton Library, 1907. The Public Libraries Act of 1892 enabled the Borough to open its first public library at 6 Cumnor Terrace. Winton Library was the first permanent one in the town and it opened in 1907. *(Russell-Cotes Art Gallery and Museum Collection/J. Barrett)*

20

Opening of East Cliff Lift, 1908. Spectators assemble for the opening ceremony of the new East Cliff Lift, performed by Lady Meyrick. *(Russell-Cotes Art Gallery and Museum Collection)*

A postcard of a watercolour by F.R. Fitzgerald, *c.* 1908. An unusual view of the East Cliff, showing the limit of the new Undercliff Drive as far as Meyrick Road and the East Cliff Lift. *(Russell-Cotes Art Gallery and Museum Collection)*

Alma Road School, 1908. In 1903 Bournemouth Education Authority met for the first time. As well as surveying existing educational provision it also began to build new schools for the expanding borough. The first of these was Alma Road School in Winton and in its first week it had 698 pupils. *(Russell-Cotes Art Gallery and Museum Collection)*

DATED FEBRUARY 1st, 1908.

MERTON RUSSELL COTES, F.R.G.S., J.P.,

AND

Mrs. RUSSELL COTES, F.R.S.L.,

TO

THE MAYOR, ALDERMEN AND BURGESSES

OF THE

BOROUGH OF BOURNEMOUTH.

DUPLICATE

LEASE AND DEED OF GIFT

OF

EAST CLIFF HALL

AND CERTAIN

ART PROPERTY CONTAINED THEREIN.

Enrolled in the Books of the Charity Commissioners for England and Wales under Section 6 of the Mortmain and Charitable Uses Act, 1888 (51 & 52, Vict. C. 42), by Order dated the Third day of March, One Thousand Nine Hundred and Eight (V. 17, p. 279).

(Signed) THOS. ALLCHIN.

In 1908 Merton and Annie Russell-Cotes signed the lease gifting their home to the people of Bournemouth, together with much of their personal collection of art and souvenirs from travels throughout the world. The gift was conditional on their continuing to live in East Cliff Hall until they died. The Russell-Cotes Art Gallery and Museum opened on 10 March 1922. *(Russell-Cotes Art Gallery and Museum Collection)*

Opening the Pier extension, 1909. George Edward Bridge, Mayor of Bournemouth and Sir George Wyatt Truscott, Lord Mayor of London on board the SS *Majestic* after the opening of the extension to the 1880 pier. The variety of headgear worn by the party is of interest and somehow a small dog has joined in the celebrations. Captain Newman, the Pier Master, looks on. *(Bournemouth Libraries)*

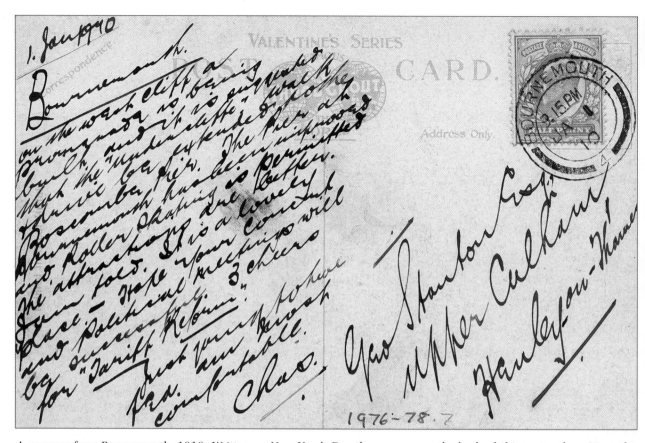

A message from Bournemouth, 1910. Written on New Year's Day the message on the back of this postcard mentions the building of the West Cliff Promenade, the improvements to the Pier and the popularity of roller-skating. This is an occasion when the message is more interesting than the picture, which shows the Upper Gardens. *(Russell-Cotes Art Gallery and Museum Collection)*

Happy Birthday Bournemouth! Bournemouth has celebrated two centenaries. The first was in 1910, 100 years after Lewis Tregonwell purchased 8½ acres of land from Sir George Tapps-Gervis on which he was to build a summer home by the sea. The second was in 1990, 100 years after the town became a municipal borough. *(Russell-Cotes Art Gallery and Museum Collection)*

Centenary aviation meeting, 1910. Bournemouth was a centre for the pioneers of aviation. A competition and display were held on open space at Southbourne to celebrate the centenary. The aviator is Graham White and the plane looks as fragile as a model made from balsa wood and tissue paper. *(Russell-Cotes Art Gallery and Museum Collection/Photochrom Company Ltd)*

Open-air treatment, *c.* 1910. The National Sanatorium opened in 1855 and was one of the first purpose-built hospitals for people suffering from chest diseases, particularly tuberculosis. In 1898 the hospital introduced a new open-air treatment where patients could benefit from fresh air, resting in outdoor shelters during the day but eventually even sleeping in them at night. Drug treatment for tuberculosis was generally available from the 1950s. *(Russell-Cotes Art Gallery and Museum Collection)*

Waterplane, 1912. Aviation displays continued to be held at Bournemouth and in 1912 enthusiasts were able to see the *Daily Mail* waterplane. A few daring individuals were lucky enough to take a ride. *(Russell-Cotes Art Gallery and Museum Collection)*

Sun, Seafront & Swimming

Seafront and Bath Hill, photographed between 1949 and 1955. This fascinating aerial photograph looks down on to a busy seafront. Some work is being carried out on the Pier. People had to cross the road with all the kit they needed for a day on the beach because the elevated roadway did not open until 1972, although on this day the roads were quite empty. There are houses between the baths and the Royal Bath Hotel as well as on the other side of the road. The Hants and Dorset bus depot is just up from the Pavilion. *(Russell-Cotes Art Gallery and Museum Collection)*

East Beach, 1912. Ninety years ago people enjoyed themselves on the beach just as we do today. The children are playing on a landing stage which allowed passengers access to and from the many pleasure boats that came to the Bay. *(Russell-Cotes Art Gallery and Museum Collection/Photograph courtesy of St Andrews University Library)*

Pier Approach, 1970s. The flyover opened in 1972, separating people and cars. The villas behind the Baths have disappeared to be replaced by a car park. The former Hants and Dorset Bus Depot was next to go. Yellow lines and road markings have appeared since the picture on page 5 was taken in 1912. *(Russell-Cotes Art Gallery and Museum Collection/Photo Precision Ltd, St Ives, Huntingdon)*

A family looks down on to the beach in 2002. There are so many things to do but one of the best must surely be simply watching all the exciting things going on. Harry Ramsden's fish and chip restaurant opened here in 1995. The aroma sometimes competes with the refreshing sea air. *(Russell-Cotes Art Gallery and Museum Collection/Martin Coyne)*

Alum Chine, 1910. Tea rooms appeared where each of the chines opened on to the beach. In 1910 the scenery at Alum Chine looks rugged and out of keeping with a developing seaside resort. It must have been a windy day judging by the state of the flag and the amount of clothes people are wearing, but then it's good to blow the cobwebs away, isn't it? *(Russell-Cotes Art Gallery and Museum Collection)*

Alum Chine, 1940s. A lot of development has taken place since 1910. An additional café, toilets and even some beach huts have appeared on the scene. It still looks windy though. *(Russell-Cotes Art Gallery and Museum Collection)*

Pokesdown, early twentieth century. The man sitting on the railings should beware. At any moment a wave could come crashing in and knock him over – but perhaps that was part of the thrill. This area is called Southbourne today, but this picture was taken before Southbourne and Boscombe boundaries met. *(Russell-Cotes Art Gallery and Museum Collection)*

Beach huts, 2002. Beach huts continue to be a significant part of seafront life for visitors and residents. They are so popular that it takes several years to get to the top of the waiting list to buy one. *(Russell-Cotes Art Gallery and Museum Collection/Martin Coyne)*

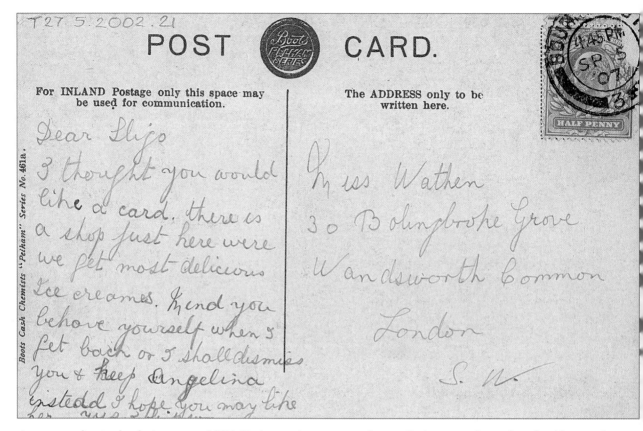

T27.5.2002.21

POST CARD.

Boots PELHAM SERIES

For INLAND Postage only this space may be used for communication.

The ADDRESS only to be written here.

Boots Cash Chemists "Pelham" Series No. 461a.

Dear Sligo

I thought you would like a card. there is a shop just here were we get most delicious ice creames. Mind you behave yourself when I get back or I shall dismiss you & keep Angelina instedd I hope you may like

Miss Wathen
30 Bolingbroke Grove
Wandsworth Common
London

S. W.

HALF PENNY

A message about a lovely ice-cream, 1907. Having an ice-cream at the seaside is one tradition that should never die out, even more so than seaside rock or candyfloss. The end of the message sounds most mysterious! *(Russell-Cotes Art Gallery and Museum Collection)*

An ice-cream on the beach, 2002. This one looks as if it is going to topple on to the sand at any moment. *(Russell-Cotes Art Gallery and Museum Collection/Martin Coyne)*

Pier Approach Baths

Bournemouth makes still another addition to its manifold attractions :

THE MAGNIFICENT NEW £80,000
PIER APPROACH BATHS

TEPID SEA WATER SWIMMING POOL
100 feet by 35 feet. 150,000 gallons of water

Depth : 3 feet to 12 feet. DIVING PIT

OLYMPIC 1 and 3 metre SPRING, and 1, 2 and 5 metre FIXED DIVING BOARDS

EXPERT INSTRUCTORS IN ATTENDANCE

LATEST TYPE OF WATER PURIFICATION INSTALLATION
ensures that the water in the Pool will, at all times, be bacteriologically pure

FREQUENT SPECIAL ATTRACTIONS IN THE POOL

WORLD-RENOWNED SWIMMERS AND DIVERS

SWIMMING CHAMPIONSHIPS, etc.

ACCOMMODATION FOR 650 SPECTATORS

SUN TERRACE AND SOLARIUM
with due South aspect

THE TURKISH AND MEDICATED BATHS OFFER EVERY MODERN FACILITY

EXPERT MASSEUR AND MASSEUSE

Pier Approach Baths. The Borough had wanted to replace the old private baths for some time and to provide customers with a modern amenity. The new baths opened in 1937. This leaflet describes all the facilities available – including a 'tepid sea water swimming pool'. *(Russell-Cotes Art Gallery and Museum Collection)*

Na-Ki-Dal Baths. Many of the leaflets exhorting people to visit the baths advertised their health benefits and tackled topics such as 'Why a Turkish bath is good for you'. This is a curious one. *(Russell-Cotes Art Gallery and Museum Collection)*

The Eight Eugene Mermaids, 1930s. These women promoted the 1930s ideal of fresh air and fitness – several of them were diving and swimming champions. They toured the country giving exhibitions and water cabarets. The troupe was sponsored by the Eugene Wave, an early form of hair 'perm' that kept their hair curly in spite of 'two or three daily immersions'. (*Russell-Cotes Art Gallery and Museum Collection*)

Pier Approach Baths, 1960s. For many years there were lots of activities at the new baths – swimming and diving displays and competitions, and exciting sports, such as water polo. Behind the Pier Approach Baths is the former Hants and Dorset bus depot, which was the Rothesay Museum until the site was redeveloped in the 1980s. (*Russell-Cotes Art Gallery and Museum Collection*)

The 1959 Aqua Show. Water cabarets were popular and an annual event throughout the 1950s and 1960s. The 1959 programme included diving exhibitions and a variety of water-based acts. *(Russell-Cotes Art Gallery and Museum Collection)*

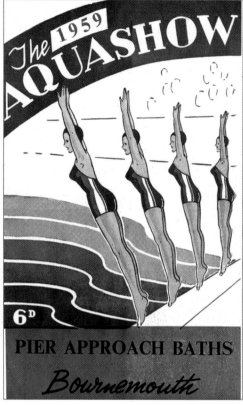

The Aquabelles, 1960s. With them is Brian Phelps, Olympic bronze medallist in 1960 and Commonwealth gold medallist in 1962 and 1966. The glamorous Aquabelles look slightly different to those on the front of the 1959 programme. The swimming caps have disappeared and bikinis have replaced the full costumes. *(Courtesy of the Daily Echo)*

Kinson Road Baths, 1970s. Other areas of Bournemouth have swimming pools, including Kinson and Stokewood Road in Charminster. *(Russell-Cotes Art Gallery and Museum Collection)*

Stokewood Road Baths, 1960s. The baths opened in 1930 and at the beginning of the Second World War the building was turned into a first aid centre. The baths have been threatened with closure on several occasions, but each time they have been saved and renovated, most recently in 1991. *(Russell-Cotes Art Gallery and Museum Collection)*

BOURNEMOUTH CORPORATION
Pier Approach Baths
WAS
Closed Down
FROM TODAY, SEPTEMBER 1st, 1984

All mail, bookings, enquiries, etc. should be directed to Stokewood Road Baths **AFTER SEPTEMBER 15th**

The Management and Staff would like to thank all those who have made use of our facilities and supported us over the years since 1937, and to express our regret that we cannot continue to serve them.

The Pier Approach Baths closed in 1984 and were demolished to make way for the redevelopment of the Pier Approach area and the construction of the Bournemouth International Centre. *(Russell-Cotes Art Gallery and Museum Collection)*

What Shall We Do Today?

A trip aboard the *Emperor of India*, 1913. Owned by Cosens & Co., this was one of several vessels providing trips around the bay and further afield to Weymouth, Torquay or even Cherbourg. The boat came into service in 1908 but before a refit it was called the *Princess Royal*. *(Russell-Cotes Art Gallery and Museum Collection)*

This cartoon by Eustace Nash, artist and observer of the local scene, suggests a strong reaction if a couple were to be caught 'spooning' on the seafront by the deckchair attendant. The dress of the young woman suggests the cartoon dates from the 1920s. *(Russell-Cotes Art Gallery and Museum Collection/Courtesy of the Estate of Eustace Nash)*

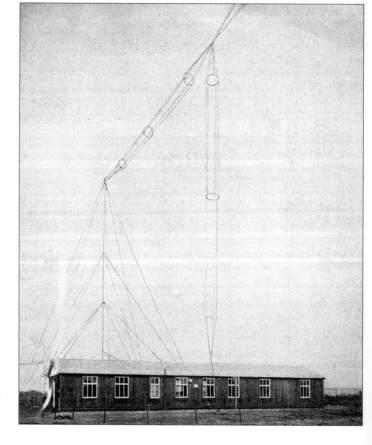

Radio transmitter, 1920s. Bournemouth was one of the first towns to have its own local radio station. The transmitting station for 6BM radio was on the site of Bushey Road and began broadcasting on 17 October 1923. At first the station carried local features, concerts and outside broadcasts, such as organ concerts from Boscombe Arcade. It also had a Children's Hour with 'Aunties' and 'Uncles' for younger listeners. *(Courtesy of George Dyke)*

George Dyke, caretaker and night watchman, polishing up the brass plate at the 6BM transmitting station, 1920s. The broadcasting studio was on the top floor of 72 Holdenhurst Road not far from 2CR FM's studios today. *(Courtesy of George Dyke)*

The staff at 6BM, 1920s. This carefully posed photograph shows some very earnest young men. In 1930 the National Programme was broadcast for the first time and later it was announced that the new transmitter for the region was to be at Start Point in Devon. The last broadcast from 6BM was on 13 June 1939. *(Courtesy of George Dyke)*

Birchmore & Lindon's Pier Pierrots, 1914. These gaily dressed men were one of the many attractions on the Pier, providing light entertainment, music and sketches. *(Russell-Cotes Art Gallery and Museum Collection)*

Birchmore & Lindon's Original Gay Cadets, 1926. The stage was set up on the Pier before the theatre was built. *(Russell-Cotes Art Gallery and Museum Collection)*

Willie Cave's Bournemouth Revels, 1934. In the days before home entertainment centres, television and computers, going out to musical shows was very popular, whether the performers were professional or amateur. The events were enjoyed by the town's visitors and residents alike. *(Russell-Cotes Art Gallery and Museum Collection)*

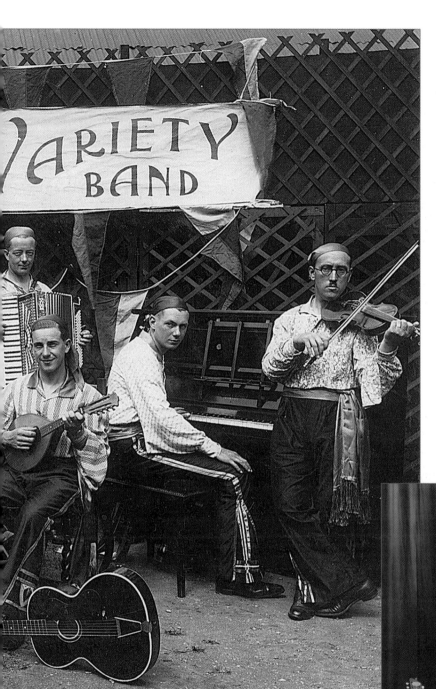

Boynton's Super Variety Band, 1937. The band played at dances all around the town. It folded at the beginning of the Second World War when its members were required for the Services. On the far left is the leader, Peter Taylor. *(Russell-Cotes Art Gallery and Museum Collection)*

Ron Palin with guitar, banjo and mandolin. He played in the Super Variety Band in his spare time; by day he worked as a clockmaker. During the Second World War Ron served in the RAF as an instrument engineer. *(Russell-Cotes Art Gallery and Museum Collection)*

Bournemouth Times & Directory, April 1939. You could go out to something different every night. Music, theatre, cinema, dance – there was so much choice. *(Russell-Cotes Art Gallery and Museum Collection)*

Bealsons v Beales football match, 1949. Norman Beale congratulates the Bealsons team on winning the Inter-business Football Championship in 1948. The score was 8–0. *(Courtesy of Beales' Archive)*

The Grand Cinema, Westbourne, *c.* 1950. This was one of many cinemas in the town; each district had at least one and Winton had three. The Grand opened in 1922 and closed in 1975. Like so many former cinemas it is now a bingo hall. Poole Road looks as busy as it is today. *(Bournemouth Libraries)*

Demolishing the Carlton Cinema, Boscombe, 2002. The Carlton opened in 1931 and closed in 1975. For a while it was a bingo and social club, but it had been derelict for several years. The site will now be redeveloped. *(Russell-Cotes Art Gallery and Museum Collection/Martin Coyne)*

Mini or crazy golf, Bournemouth Lower Gardens, 1960s. Crazy golf is one of those games that everyone has played at least once while on holiday. The deckchairs are out ready for a concert at the bandstand and people are strolling around. *(Russell-Cotes Art Gallery and Museum Collection/Photo Precision Ltd, St Ives, Huntingdon)*

Mini golf, Bournemouth Lower Gardens, 2002. Mini golf is as popular as ever and on some days there are queues at the entrance hut and at each tee. *(Russell-Cotes Art Gallery and Museum Collection/Martin Coyne)*

Beatlemania comes to Bournemouth, August 1964. This is the back entrance to the Gaumont in Gervis Road. Where is Ringo, and with all the screaming girls did the young man on the right stand a chance of getting an autograph? *(Courtesy of the Daily Echo)*

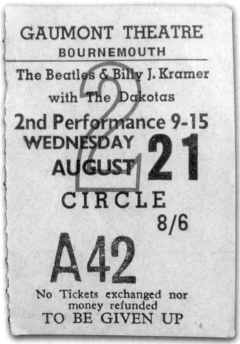

Beatles' concert ticket, 1964. It cost 8s 6d for a seat at the front of the circle, that's about 42p in today's money. The Gaumont was originally the Regent and became the Odeon in 1986. *(Courtesy of the Daily Echo)*

Cliff Richard outside the studios of 2CR FM, 1995. Cliff has been a regular visitor to Bournemouth, much to the delight of his fans. 2CR FM, Bournemouth's local radio station, has its studios in Southcote Road. (*Courtesy of the Daily Echo*)

Waiting for the eclipse, August 1999. This was to be the one big chance to see a total eclipse of the sun in England for decades. For weeks before the event the media was full of advice on how to avoid damaging your eyes and also provided free spectacles. The best views were to be had in Cornwall but that didn't stop lots of people trekking up to Hengistbury Head. Unfortunately on the day it was very overcast and there was very little to see. (*Courtesy of the Daily Echo*)

Ladysmith Black Mambazo, 2002. National and international artists perform in Bournemouth. The ten members of Ladysmith Black Mambazo from South Africa were photographed outside the Pavilion in June 2002. *(Louise Perrin)*

Tickets for the concert were £22.50. How does this compare with 8s 6d for The Beatles' performance in 1964? *(Louise Perrin)*

51

Surfing, 2002. Surfing is a popular activity on Bournemouth seafront. Although the waves are never really spectacular, conditions offer a chance to practise, particularly to develop the skill of falling off boards and getting on again. Surfers can often be seen in the early morning and look like black ants in the water. *(Louise Perrin)*

Jet skiing, 2002. Fast, furious and a lot of fun. *(Russell-Cotes Art Gallery and Museum Collection/Martin Coyne)*

Hen party, 2002. Bournemouth is a popular venue for stag and hen parties. On Friday and Saturday nights in the centre of town they are easy to spot, often dressed up in crazy costumes and having a great time before the serious business of getting married. *(Russell-Cotes Art Gallery and Museum Collection/Martin Coyne)*

Bournemouth Symphony Orchestra

Concert programme, 1904. The front cover of a programme for a performance on the Pier by Dan Godfrey and the Municipal Orchestra. During the summer season a full military band played from 11.15 to 12.45 every morning. A smaller band played in the evenings from 7.30 to 9.30. *(Russell-Cotes Art Gallery and Museum Collection/BSO Archive)*

The Winter Gardens, *c.* 1900.
This was a spectacular glass
pavilion but the acoustics were
not very good. The first Winter
Gardens opened in 1877 and
were converted into a concert
hall in 1893. The building was
dismantled in 1935 when the
Bournemouth Municipal
Orchestra was already playing
at the newly built Pavilion.
*(Russell-Cotes Art Gallery and
Museum Collection/BSO Archive)*

Dan Godfrey, founder-conductor of the Bournemouth Municipal Orchestra, and company, 1920s. Most photographs of Dan Godfrey show him looking rather serious but here he is in a lighter mood having a good time with colleagues on the Pier. He was awarded a knighthood in 1922 for his services to music. He is especially noted for his performances of new works by contemporary English composers. *(Russell-Cotes Art Gallery and Museum Collection/BSO Archive)*

Three members of the Bournemouth Municipal Orchestra stepping out along the pier on their way to a rehearsal, 1920. *(Russell-Cotes Art Gallery and Museum Collection/BSO Archive)*

Sir Dan Godfrey, 1930s. An unusual photograph of Dan Godfrey sitting in a deckchair, possibly at Alum Chine near to where he lived. Although he is sitting on the beach, he is still wearing a suit. Sir Dan retired in 1934 and died in 1939. *(Russell-Cotes Art Gallery and Museum Collection/BSO Archive)*

Bournemouth Municipal Orchestra, 1951. A typical photograph of the orchestra and chorus in 1951 after a performance of Beethoven's Mass in D. During the war the orchestra had been reduced from sixty-one to twenty-four players. A year after this photograph was taken it was suggested that the orchestra merge with the City of Birmingham Symphony Orchestra. In 1954 its name was changed to the Bournemouth Symphony Orchestra. *(Russell-Cotes Art Gallery and Museum Collection/BSO Archive/Arthur Coleman, Boscombe)*

Bournemouth Symphonic Brass, 2002. Five members of the Bournemouth Symphony Orchestra play near the Pier as part of the Borough Council's arts development programme, 'Creating Community Through The Arts'. At the beginning of the twenty-first century local companies are still advertising pleasure trips and evening cruises. *(Russell-Cotes Art Gallery and Museum Collection)*

Transport, Roads
& Town Development

Aerial photograph of Bournemouth, 13 August 1982. This stunning picture clearly shows the impact of the car in the twentieth century, but the legacy of nineteenth-century tree planting is still in evidence. The Travel Interchange and the Asda superstore have yet to appear but the land has been cleared for the Bournemouth International Centre. *(Courtesy of the Daily Echo/Kitchenham Ltd – Bournemouth, 01202 513387)*

The Square, *c.* 1908. The Empress Hotel at the bottom of Richmond Hill closed between 1952 and 1955, when the National Provincial Bank took over the building. Why is there a watering can in the centre of the picture? *(Russell-Cotes Art Gallery and Museum Collection)*

The first electric tramway ran from Pokesdown to the Lansdowne and was opened in 1902, to be followed by the Poole to Boscombe line in 1903. Laying all the tracks must have been a major undertaking. This photograph may show the re-laying of the Poole line in 1925 or the Lower Parkstone line in 1926. *(Russell-Cotes Art Gallery and Museum Collection)*

Car 13 Bournemouth Corporation tram to Boscombe. The driver and the conductor look very proud. *(Russell-Cotes Art Gallery and Museum Collection)*

Traffic congestion, Old Christchurch Road. What an assortment of vehicles – a trolleybus, a tram with cyclists alongside and a car behind, all bumper to bumper, and no bus lanes then! This photograph was taken during the transition from trams to trolleybuses while both systems operated alongside each other. *(Russell-Cotes Art Gallery and Museum Collection)*

Bournemouth Transport centenary, 2002. An open-top 'yellow bus' in Avenue Road celebrating 100 years of Bournemouth Transport and proudly advertising the new 'low floor' which allows easier access. This is the route 12 coastal service to Christchurch. *(Russell-Cotes Art Gallery and Museum Collection/Martin Coyne)*

Bournemouth West station, 1965. From 1874 Bournemouth West received passengers from Poole and the West Country. It was connected to Bournemouth East station (now Central station) and the main Brockenhurst–Southampton line in 1888. The station closed in 1965 and was demolished in 1970. The cars are interesting too. Is that a Simca in the middle of the three? *(Courtesy of the Daily Echo)*

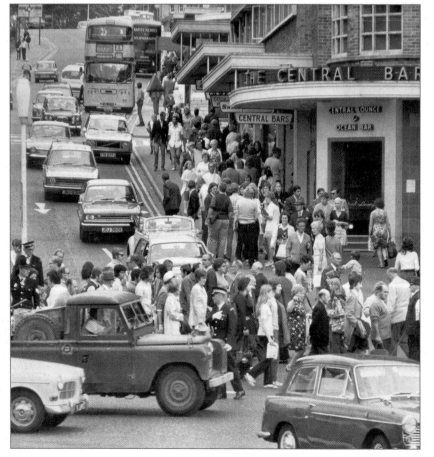

The junction of Richmond Hill and The Square, 1971. Cars, buses, and people are all trying to get to their destination – a lethal combination. A police officer is directing the pedestrians and two traffic wardens are trying to assist. Early opponents of pedestrianisation said it would lead to a reduction in trade. These days Bournemouth on a Saturday disproves that theory. *(Courtesy of the Daily Echo)*

Constructing the Richmond Hill underpass, October 1976. The construction of Wessex Way was another of Bournemouth's major engineering projects; it necessitated the compulsory purchase of land and property, and was phased in over several years. Before Wessex Way was built there had been a simple roundabout here. *(Courtesy of the Daily Echo)*

Richmond Hill underpass, 2002. Twenty-five years later the traffic roars by underneath and people can walk safely across the road. The scars caused by the roadworks have disappeared and the area is landscaped. *(Russell-Cotes Art Gallery and Museum/ Martin Coyne)*

J.E. Badger's shop, Wimborne Road, 1962. Badger was a newsagent, stationer and, judging by all the adverts, a tobacconist, selling brands that have long since disappeared such as Woodbines, Senior Service, Wills' Capstan (full strength). There is also a chewing gum machine on the outside wall. The shop was opposite Winton police station near the junction with Jameson Road. *(Bournemouth Libraries/Kitchenham Ltd – Bournemouth, 01202 513387)*

Wimborne Road, 1962. Evening rush hour traffic at the junction of Wimborne Road with Bryanstone Road. The cyclists are weaving their way between the parked and moving vehicles. *(Bournemouth Libraries)*

Brightly coloured, modern shop frontages beneath the Victorian and Edwardian upper storeys in Wimborne Road, Winton, 1990s. The shops are all branches of chains found across suburban England, such as Currys, SupaSnaps, Victoria Wine and Going Places. And just like every shopping centre it has a variety of charity shops, such as Scope. *(Bournemouth Libraries)*

Hume Towers, Branksome Wood Road, 1966. This magnificent house was built in 1871 for Sir Joshua Walmsley. The architect was Christopher Crabbe Creeke. Sadly Sir Joshua died a few months after moving in and his wife not long afterwards. After several changes of ownership it was bought in 1899 by the Hon William Earnshaw Cooper. He died in 1924 and like so many of Bournemouth's grand houses it later became a private convalescent home. *(Bournemouth Libraries)*

Hume Towers, nineteenth century. This picture of the library comes from a sale brochure and each room is described in the most effusive and glowing terms. The interior décor was the most luxurious of its day. *(Bournemouth Libraries)*

Hume Towers, 1966. It is always sad to see such a glorious house demolished, but there is often no alternative. Large old houses frequently do not make good nursing homes, or museums, which need modern facilities and good access. The redeveloped site provided homes for many people. *(Bournemouth Libraries)*

Townsend Cottages, Holdenhurst, 1969. The need for the A338 spur road was anticipated very early in the century. When it was completed, the dual carriageway ran just outside several people's back doors. This farming village, which dates back to before the Domesday survey, was split in two, with some of its fields now on the opposite side of the road to the houses. *(Private Collection)*

Townsend Barn, 2002. The houses were destroyed by fire in 1991 and all that remains is the barn. Just beyond the barn is the famous crossing where the farmer stops the traffic to move his cattle to his fields on the other side of the road. A park and ride scheme is being considered for this area. *(Louise Perrin)*

Iford, Hampshire, *c.* 1900. Until the twentieth century, Iford was a rural hamlet between Christchurch and Bournemouth and a crossing place for the River Stour. There has been a bridge at Iford since the twelfth century. *(Russell-Cotes Art Gallery and Museum Collection)*

Iford, 2002. There is little remaining of the farming hamlet of Iford in the present settlement. Iford was incorporated into Bournemouth at the beginning of the twentieth century. In neither Dorset nor Hampshire now, it is part of the Bournemouth Unitary Authority. *(Louise Perrin)*

Cartoon by Eustace Nash, 1914. This is a topical comment of the day about the Borough's plans for expansion. The tall man is surely James Cooper Dean who was so concerned about the spread of Bournemouth right up to his doorstep that he bought a large part of the Iford Estate when it came up for sale in 1898. The man at the head of the group on the left is the Town Clerk, Mr Herbert Ashling, and to the left in the hat, white suit and bow tie is the mayor, Dr Henry Seymour McCalmont Hill. With them are members of the Borough Extension and Ward Redistribution Committee. *(Russell-Cotes Art Gallery and Museum Collection/Courtesy of the Estate of Eustace Nash)*

People &
Communities

Unknown soldier, 1916. This young man, smartly dressed in his clean uniform, is posing proudly in the photographer's studio. What is the link with Bournemouth? The photograph was taken by Emmett & Co, 261 Christchurch Road, Boscombe. *(Russell-Cotes Art Gallery and Museum Collection)*

Disabled Sailors' and Soldiers' Workshops, 1927. The workshops were set up after the First World War to provide employment for eighteen disabled ex-servicemen. When the Prince of Wales (later briefly Edward VIII and then Duke of Windsor) made an official visit to Bournemouth in 1927 this was one of the places he saw. *(Russell-Cotes Art Gallery and Museum Collection)*

Advert for the Disabled Sailors' and Soldiers' Workshops inside a Bournemouth tram. *(Russell-Cotes Art Gallery and Museum Collection)*

918 Company (TA) Royal Army Service Corps marching through Bournemouth, 1939. The company was formed of volunteers in the week before war was declared. Most of its members were from Bournemouth, Poole and Christchurch and several had links with the motor trade. The Commanding Officer was Major Rogers of the Territorial Army. 918 Company saw active service in the Middle East, North Africa and Italy. *(Russell-Cotes Art Gallery and Museum Collection)*

A sign declares Father Christmas is to arrive by aeroplane, *c.* 1912. It is believed that the Beales' Father Christmas (aka Cyril Beale) was the first ever to arrive by plane. From the look of the upstairs windows, rocking horses were a popular choice for Christmas presents. *(Courtesy of Beales' Archive)*

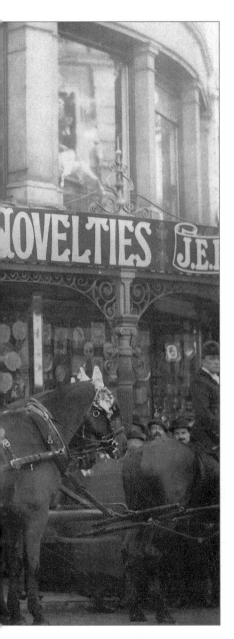

Beales' Father Christmas parade, late 1950s. The parades were an annual feature in Bournemouth for most of the twentieth century up to 1989. All the town centre streets were closed for the procession. These jolly cellos are coming down Bath Hill. *(Courtesy of Beales' Archive)*

Bath Hill. The jolly cellos parade down Bath Hill past the Russell Court Hotel. The influence of television on the costumes can be seen by the presence of Bill, Ben and Little Weed. *(Courtesy of Beales' Archive)*

Malmesbury Park School, 1920s. Malmesbury Park School opened in 1901 but moved to Lowther Road in 1972 when the original school was demolished to make way for Wessex Way. Ron Palin and Fred Skinner are third and fourth from the right on the front row and were friends all the way through school. *(Courtesy of Ron Palin)*

Malmesbury Park School, 1920s. Although this photograph was taken only a few years later than the one above the contrast between the two seems quite marked. Fred Skinner is on the left-hand end of the back row and Ron Palin is next to him. *(Courtesy of Ron Palin)*

Malmesbury Park School, 2002. The school reached its century in 2001 but decided to celebrate in 2002 to tie in with Queen Elizabeth's Golden Jubilee. Seen the day before the celebrations, these children from year 3 have arranged themselves like the children in the earlier photographs. *(Russell-Cotes Art Gallery and Museum Collection/Martin Coyne)*

Fred Skinner, 1941. Fred joined the army just before the start of the Second World War. He was killed in 1944 not long after he was married. *(Courtesy of Ron Palin)*

A Victory in Europe (VE Day) street party, 1945. While many soldiers had come home, Ron Palin was still in the Far East waiting for demobilisation and was involved in the RAF Mutiny in India in January 1946. More than 50,000 airmen serving in India and the Far East mounted strikes protesting about the slowness of demobilisation and the state of service conditions when the war had been over for several months. Back at home Ron's son Terry was able to join in the fun with his grandma. *(Courtesy of Ron Palin)*

'Prefab', Mallard Road, 1947. Bombing raids destroyed many homes and to cope with the housing shortage the government built prefabs. In 1947 Mr and Mrs Palin moved into their new home in Mallard Road, where the bus depot is now. At the time it seemed very well-appointed accommodation with all the modern features a family would need to make themselves comfortable. The house was called 'Palkathron', a title made up from their names, Ron and Kath Palin. Mrs Palin is sitting on the doorstep with the couple's daughter Genevieve. *(Courtesy of Ron Palin)*

Ibbertson Road, 1952. The Palin family were later allocated a council house and moved to Ibbertson Road just across the other side of Castle Lane. *(Courtesy of Ron Palin)*

Bournemouth seafront, 19 May 1964. Confrontations between Mods (scooters and parkas) and Rockers (motorbikes and leather) flared up briefly in south coast seaside resorts in the mid-1960s, although Bournemouth was not affected to the same extent as Brighton, Broadstairs or Margate. This gathering of young people shows an interesting variety of dress styles, including winklepickers and cardigans. *(Courtesy of the Daily Echo)*

Holdenhurst Road, 1986. A windy day in 1986 resulted in this dramatic scene when scaffolding fell on to parked cars in Holdenhurst Road. A woman and her daughter were driving past when the accident happened, but fortunately they escaped serious injury, nor were any pedestrians hurt. *(Courtesy of the Daily Echo)*

Leeson Road and Littledown Avenue, 1991. It does occasionally snow in Bournemouth. When people woke up on the morning of 27 February 1991 they discovered it had snowed overnight. The snow had turned to slush on busy Littledown Avenue but the side roads and pavements were still covered. *(Courtesy of the Daily Echo)*

Bournemouth
at Work

HÔTEL BURLINGTON,
BOSCOMBE, . . .
BOURNEMOUTH.   .

Hôtel Burlington, 1898. This advert for the Burlington Hotel comes from *Bright's Illustrated Guide to Bournemouth*, 1901. Boscombe Pier looks minuscule in comparison with the hotel and the whole picture has a very continental appearance, an impression emphasised by the use of the circumflex over the 'o' in Hôtel. The hotel opened in 1888. *(Bournemouth Libraries)*

Hôtel Burlington, *c.* 1915. The architect was Thomas Edward Colcutt who also designed the Savoy Hotel in London and was a president of the RIBA. During the 1950s and 1960s there were various planning applications to convert it into flats including one to demolish the hotel and build a thirteen-storey block. It is now a Grade II listed building. *(Russell-Cotes Art Gallery and Museum Collection)*

Burlington Mansions, 2002. The east and west wings of the hotel were converted into apartments at the end of the twentieth century but the remaining central section continued to operate as a hotel until 2001. This section is now being turned into apartments too. *(Russell-Cotes Art Gallery and Museum Collection/Martin Coyne)*

Bournemouth Steam Laundry, 1888. An early advert states that the laundry was capable of 'doing from Thirty to Forty Thousand articles per week'. It was situated next to the East station (now Central station) on Holdenhurst Road and closed in the 1980s. *(Russell-Cotes Art Gallery and Museum Collection)*

Steam Laundry, *c.* 1900. In all its years of operation the laundry rarely undertook work for the hotel trade because it did not provide consistent year-round business. Customers' laundry was collected and delivered by a fleet of horse-drawn wagons. William Clapcott Dean's name appears on a fire insurance certificate in 1876. He was related to the Cooper-Dean family who were to have such a significant effect on the face of Bournemouth. *(Russell-Cotes Art Gallery and Museum Collection)*

Steam Laundry pressing room, *c.* 1900. Women were employed in the pressing room to iron, press and fold everything from small garments to large items of linen. The overhead line shafts were powered by steam and drove the rotary pressing machines. *(Russell-Cotes Art Gallery and Museum Collection)*

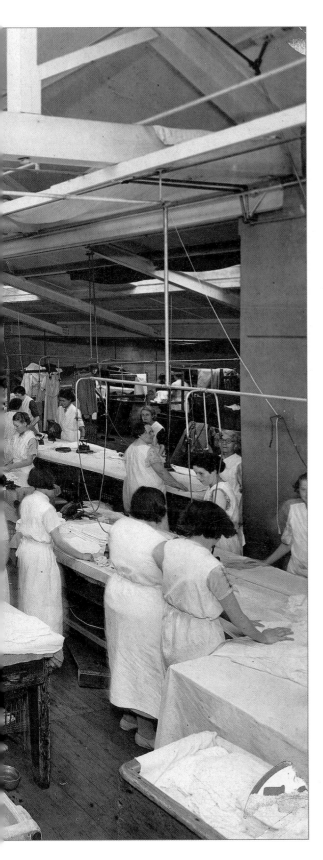

Steam Laundry, 1930s. By this time the pressing room was powered by electricity supplied from overhead cables. The work still looks very hard and tiring on the legs. *(Russell-Cotes Art Gallery and Museum Collection)*

Steam Laundry, 1930s. It was important that the laundry remain up-to-date, as this fleet of delivery vans with smartly dressed drivers shows. *(Russell-Cotes Art Gallery and Museum Collection)*

Bill Palin, 1922. Doorstep milk deliveries were a feature of the twentieth century and the design of the milkcart and the outfit of the milkman help to show the passage of time. *(Courtesy of Ron Palin)*

Bill Palin, *c.* 1935. Mr Palin worked for the Malmesbury & Parsons Dairies. In the previous photograph he is still carrying a churn. While the style of his cart had not changed much by the time this picture was taken, the milk was now being delivered in bottles. *(Courtesy of Ron Palin)*

Bill Palin, 1960s. Malmesbury & Parsons was formed in 1918. It was the only local dairy in the early part of the century to pasteurise milk. An outbreak of typhoid in 1936 was traced to contaminated milk from another firm and as a result all local dairies were required to pasteurise their milk. The company was taken over by Unigate in 1970. *(Courtesy of Ron Palin)*

J.J. Allen Ltd, *c.* 1900. J.J. Allen was one of Bournemouth's major department stores. It was situated over the road from St Peter's Church on the corner of Hinton Road opposite Beales. *(Courtesy of the Estate of Dennis Dowding)*

J.J. Allen Ltd. Like many department and furnishing stores, Allen's was also involved in house removals and storage. While the house behind appears twentieth century, the removal vehicle definitely looks Victorian! *(Courtesy of the Estate of Dennis Dowding)*

J.J. Allen Ltd, 1930s. The shop was updated in the 1920s and its position on the corner of Hinton Road and St Peter's Road is more apparent. A piece of ironwork on Beales' store is visible at the bottom left corner of the photo. *(Courtesy of the Estate of Dennis Dowding)*

Dingles store, 1970s. J.J. Allen Ltd was eventually taken over by House of Fraser and for a while the old antiques department was incorporated into the new store. *(Courtesy of the Estate of Dennis Dowding)*

Letter-box, 2002. There has been a letter-box on this spot for over 100 years. It can be seen in the picture of J.J. Allen Ltd on page 91, and in the photo of bomb damaged Beales on page 113. *(Russell-Cotes Art Gallery and Museum Collection/Martin Coyne)*

The 'Cleveland' Mobile Canteen, 1940s. This is an interesting example of one of Bournemouth's other businesses. There must have been many occasions when it was a very welcome sight. *(Russell-Cotes Art Gallery and Museum Collection)*

A rare photograph of Bournemouth Libraries' bookbinding department, Winton, 1970s. At one time every library service had its own bindery, usually with a master-binder and several staff. Today the bindery at Winton deals mainly with book repairs and has only one part-time member of staff. (*Bournemouth Libraries*)

Royal Bath Hotel, *c.* 1900. At first glance the Royal Bath does not look any different today, plus or minus a few trees, but notice that the road and pavements are not properly made up. (*Russell-Cotes Art Gallery and Museum Collection*)

Staff ball, Royal Bath Hotel, 1920s. While the men in 'black tie' could be from almost any era, the women are very clearly in 1920s fashions. The short dresses and bobbed hairstyles must have seemed very daring, and yet they are being worn here by women of all ages. Shorter skirts meant that stockings were more visible but women had to wait until the 1960s for the convenience of tights. *(Russell-Cotes Art Gallery and Museum Collection)*

Salisbury Bedroom, Royal Bath Hotel, 1890s. This luxuriously appointed bedroom was arranged with some of the souvenirs brought back from their foreign travels by the hotel's owner Merton Russell-Cotes and his wife Annie. Some of the objects in this photograph are now on display in the Russell-Cotes Art Gallery and Museum. *(Russell-Cotes Art Gallery and Museum Collection)*

Royal Bath Hotel, 1959. Even its commanding position on Bath Hill did not stop the Royal Bath Hotel from being affected by the appearance of the overhead wiring for the trolleybuses. Street lighting and bollards have appeared by 1959, and cars are parked on the road in front of the hotel – no yellow lines then, though. *(Russell-Cotes Art Gallery and Museum Collection/Kitchenham Ltd – Bournemouth, 01202 513387)*

Phyllis Stebbing, *c.* 1913. Phyllis was the daughter of Ella and Edward Stebbing, and the grand-daughter of Merton and Annie Russell-Cotes. In 1932, Phyllis Lee-Duncan, as she was by then, took over the running of the Royal Bath Hotel from her uncle, Herbert Russell-Cotes, who himself had assumed control when Merton died in 1921. *(Russell-Cotes Art Gallery and Museum Collection)*

Phyllis Lee-Duncan (second from the left), 1940. During the Second World War the Royal Bath Hotel, like so many others in Bournemouth, was requisitioned for military use. The hotel provided accommodation for Canadian officers while continuing to offer 'service as usual' for other visitors. The hotel remained within the family until 1963 when Mrs Lee-Duncan sold it, although at one point she had thought of turning it into flats. *(Russell-Cotes Art Gallery and Museum Collection)*

Buildings & Landmarks

The Avenue, 1920s. This road was the entrance driveway to Branksome Towers. Early guides to Bournemouth included Branksome Chine and Branksome Towers, although both are in Poole. The boundary between Poole and Bournemouth was also the boundary between Dorset and Hampshire. Following local government reorganisation in 1974 Bournemouth became part of Dorset, and The Avenue is now the border between Poole and Bournemouth. The view is not dissimilar in 2002 although many of the large houses have been demolished and replaced by large blocks of flats. *(Russell-Cotes Art Gallery and Museum Collection)*

The Pavilion opened in 1929 on the site of the old Belle Vue Hotel. It had been planned before 1900 and at times it looked as though Bournemouth would never acquire a multi-purpose venue. The development was very controversial and arguments moved back and forth between proposers and opposers. However, it is now entering its second century as one of the town's major centres of entertainment. *(Russell-Cotes Art Gallery and Museum Collection/J. Reade Technical Photographers Ltd)*

Bournemouth Pier. The postcard is dated 1925 but the men's uniforms suggest it was taken during the First World War. The man and woman in the centre are having a very animated conversation. *(Russell-Cotes Art Gallery and Museum Collection)*

Bournemouth Pier, 1947. During the Second World War a section of the Pier was demolished to make it inaccessible to the enemy who might land here and gain access to the shore. After the war the gap was filled in again. *(Russell-Cotes Art Gallery and Museum Collection)*

Lower Gardens, *c.* 1910. This view shows a formal flower bedding and a fountain where the Bournemouth Eye balloon is today. Bournemouth has always been proud of its gardens and floral displays. In recent years it has regularly won the Southern England in Bloom competition, and took the Britain in Bloom title in 1992, 1994 and 1995. *(Russell-Cotes Art Gallery and Museum Collection)*

Lower Gardens, *c.* 1939. A few decades later and the gardens look more luxurious and rather tropical. The skyline has changed as well. The top of the Pavilion is visible and a large block of flats has appeared. *(Russell-Cotes Art Gallery and Museum Collection)*

The Square, 1918. The Square was widened in 1899 and a small island added in the centre. The new century was eighteen years old when this picture was taken but The Square manages to look quite Victorian, even though the trams and cars show this is definitely a later date. The Square was soon to be altered once more to include a rectangular bus depot and a clock tower. *(Russell-Cotes Art Gallery and Museum Collection)*

The Square, 1970s. The tram lines have been replaced by trolleybus wires. The bus depot has given way to a large floral roundabout which retains the clock tower as its centrepiece. *(Russell-Cotes Art Gallery and Museum Collection)*

Boscombe, of course, had its own pier which opened in 1889. Piers were originally landing stages for steamers but they later developed as places to enjoy fresh air, gentle exercise and even 'end of the pier' theatres. *(Russell-Cotes Art Gallery and Museum Collection)*

Roller-skating on Boscombe Pier, *c.* 1910. People partaking of gentle exercise must have been thoroughly alarmed by young men on roller-skates enjoying the latest craze from America. Curiously, one of the three men on the left is carrying a saw. *(Russell-Cotes Art Gallery and Museum Collection)*

A roller-skating exhibition. Several arenas were set up for public use and for demonstrations by roller-skating experts. The public could skate at the Winter Gardens on Thursday evenings and all day Friday, on Bournemouth Pier from 2.30–10pm and at Boscombe Pier, daily until 10pm. Bands often played at the same time. *(Russell-Cotes Art Gallery and Museum Collection)*

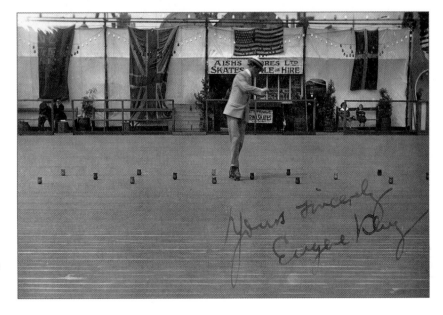

Branksome New Drive, Bournemouth, *c.* 1908. This was to become West Overcliff Drive and the photograph shows it before the rhododendrons grew and large houses sprang up. The road layout is exactly the same today. The beginnings of Milner Road can be seen on the right. *(Russell-Cotes Art Gallery and Museum Collection)*

West Overcliff Drive, 1910. Only a few years later and large houses have appeared, although the area is not looking as elegant as it was later to become. In 2002 it is almost impossible to see the houses for all the greenery. *(Russell-Cotes Art Gallery and Museum Collection)*

The past is all around us. So many people must have sent their seaside postcards from this Victorian letter-box on Meyrick Road and continue to do so. *(Louise Perrin)*

The Imperial Hotel. This grand Victorian hotel was located at the Lansdowne on the corner of Meyrick Road and Bath Hill. The man with the bath chairs appears not to have had any customers for some time. *(Russell-Cotes Art Gallery and Museum Collection)*

The main entrance to the Herbert Home, a convalescent home for patients from Salisbury Infirmary, early twentieth century. It was built within the Alum Cliff Estate and opened in 1867. Today it is a residential and day care centre for people with mental health problems. *(Russell-Cotes Art Gallery and Museum Collection)*

The convalescent home was designed according to the ideas of Florence Nightingale. In the 1920s a leaflet sent out with information for patients suggested that if they wished they could bring their own eggs for boiling. *(Bournemouth Libraries)*

Beales' Oriental House, *c.* 1900. John Elmes Beale opened his first shop at 3 St Peter's Terrace in 1881, selling 'fancy goods'. The Fancy Fair became the Oriental House in the 1890s. At the time of this photograph the store had begun to sell fabrics, and Liberty fabrics were the height of fashion. *(Courtesy of Beales' Archive)*

Rebuilding the store. The north section of Beales was completely rebuilt in 1931. Something very interesting must be happening for so many people to be peering over the edge. *(Courtesy of Beales' Archive)*

Beales' new store, a magnificent Art Deco building, 1931. *(Courtesy of Beales' Archive)*

An anti-aircraft gunner on the lookout from the roof of Beales' building. *(Courtesy of Beales' Archive)*

Beales, bomb damaged, 23 May 1943. Around lunchtime on Sunday 23 May there was a major air raid, many people were killed and many homes and businesses were destroyed. Beales' store suffered a direct hit. J.J. Allen next door was damaged as well, although the letter-box somehow survived. *(Courtesy of Beales' Archive)*

EAST CLIFF HALL
THE RUSSELL-COTES ART GALLERY AND MUSEUM

East Cliff Hall is arguably the last Victorian house to be built in Bournemouth. It is certainly one of the most spectacular. Completed in 1901, it was the cliff-top residence of Merton and Annie Russell-Cotes, who owned the Royal Bath Hotel. During the twentieth century it saw many changes, not least the transition from private residence to public museum. The Russell-Cotes announced in 1907 that Annie would give the house and much of its contents, and Merton a large part of his art collection, to the people of Bournemouth, on condition that they could continue living in their home during their lifetimes. At first the house was open to the public for one afternoon per week, but the Russell-Cotes Art Gallery and Museum was officially opened to the public on 10 March 1922.

There have been many changes. Even while Merton and Annie were alive three art galleries were added to the east of the house, opening in 1919. A fourth art gallery was completed in 1926. During the Second World War many of the museum's works of art were removed for safe keeping, which is just as well because the building suffered some damage from the blast of a parachute mine dropped by a single German bomber on 7 October 1941. Up until the 1960s it was a condition of employment that the curators and their families 'live-in', occupying the rooms in the basement of the house. A modern extension was added to the west side of the building in 1989 providing additional display space for the museum's growing collection.

After 100 years of wear and tear on the exposed cliff-top, the museum required something more than routine maintenance and recently underwent a £3 million renovation project funded by Bournemouth Borough Council and a grant from the Heritage Lottery Fund. In addition to unglamorous but essential building work, the project included the restoration of the interior décor, returning the building to how it would have appeared in 1921 after Merton died. A lot of the decorative work was based on extensive research using original photographs, documentary and oral evidence. In some cases, evidence of original designs and colour schemes was discovered when wall-mounted display cases were removed. The gardens have also been restored, including the important Japanese-style 'cloud clipped' hedge of holm oaks.

The Russell-Cotes Art Gallery and Museum was formally reopened to the public by the Duke of Gloucester on 11 September 2001. The museum begins its second century with a range of permanent displays and changing exhibitions to suit all visitors, a light and stylish craft café, and many of the features expected in a modern visitor facility. At its core remain the home and collections of its founders, Sir Merton Russell-Cotes and Lady Russell-Cotes, in all their eccentric, glittering and idiosyncratic glory.

Building East Cliff Hall. This detailed image is taken from a much larger photograph of the Bournemouth Regatta. It is an important picture because it is the only known image showing work in progress on East Cliff Hall between 1898 and 1901. *(Bournemouth Libraries)*

East Cliff Hall, 1903–7. At the end of the twentieth century the Russell-Cotes Art Gallery and Museum underwent a major restoration project funded by Bournemouth Borough Council and a grant from the Heritage Lottery fund. The museum and gardens have been restored to how they would have been in 1921 at the time of Merton's death, including the wonderful striped canopies above the windows. *(Russell-Cotes Art Gallery and Museum Collection/AATW)*

War memorial and art gallery extension, 1926. The Russell-Cotes added three art galleries to their home, all of which opened in 1919. A fourth gallery was added in an odd-shaped plot at the eastern side of the house in 1926. This gallery was built by Herbert and Ella Russell-Cotes after there parents had died, and in accordance with their parents' wishes. *(Russell Cotes Art Gallery and Museum Collection)*

The gnome garden, 1937. Until the 1960s the curators and their families lived on the premises. Joy and her sister Faith were the daughters of Norman Silvester, and each had their own little garden. While Joy liked flowers, Faith (on the left) had a gnome garden. During the recent restoration of the museum's garden, a little gnome was found at the bottom of one of the ponds. *(Russell-Cotes Art Gallery and Museum Collection/photograph by Norman Silvester)*

Ice-skating on the terrace, January 1941. Norman Silvester and his family were keen ice-skaters. During the war when the ice rink was closed, Mr Silvester, obviously a very inventive man, laid clay on the gravel of the terrace and with help from a water spray and an overnight frost was able to produce a skating rink for everyone to enjoy. *(Russell-Cotes Art Gallery and Museum Collection/photograph by Norman Silvester)*

Geological Terrace. The war memorial was removed in 1950 because it was becoming dangerous due to the erosion of the limestone. It was replaced by the Geological Terrace, an idea of the then curator, Norman Silvester. He collected geological specimens, many donated by quarrying firms, and arranged them chronologically on the site of the war memorial. The Geological Terrace itself was removed in 1997 during the most recent restoration project because the gardens were being returned to their original appearance. The samples are in store awaiting a new home within the Borough. *(Russell-Cotes Art Gallery and Museum Collection)*

Russell-Cotes Art Gallery and Museum, 1997. The restoration programme meant that the museum had to be closed and all its contents packed away for safe keeping. However, when display cases were moved, details of previous decorating schemes were discovered and details of stencil work. These have all been restored. *(Russell-Cotes Art Gallery and Museum Collection/James Howe)*

Russell-Cotes Art Gallery and Museum, 2001. The Mikado's Room shows many of the items that Annie and Merton brought back from their trip to Japan in 1885. This way of displaying the objects reflects contemporary photographs of their Japanese drawing room in the Royal Bath Hotel. *(Russell-Cotes Art Gallery and Museum Collection/James Howe)*

Ready to face another 100 years. The Russell-Cotes Art Gallery and Museum in 2002 following the restoration of the exterior and gardens. *(Russell-Cotes Art Gallery and Museum Collection/Mandy Schaller)*

Looking to the Future

Building Bournemouth International Centre, 1970s. The centre is a major conference, leisure and entertainment venue for residents and for visitors. Before the mammoth building project could get under way many of the old hotels and guest houses on the West Cliff had to be demolished. *(Russell-Cotes Art Gallery and Museum Collection)*

Court Royal, 1947. The Court Royal was one building that escaped the bulldozer. It was originally the Madeira Hotel, the site from which Marconi sent some of his early telegraph messages. The development of the telegraph enabled the murderer Dr Crippen to be arrested while at sea. There is a further Bournemouth connection to the infamous doctor: his mistress Ethel le Neve, who was with him on board ship, later came to live in Iford. *(Trustees of the Royal Court Convalescent Home for the South Wales Mining Industry)*

In 1947 the hotel reopened as the Court Royal, a convalescent home for miners from South Wales, and continues to provide the same service today, although the miners are now allowed to bring their wives at certain times of the year. *(Trustees of the Royal Court Convalescent Home for the South Wales Mining Industry)*

Sculpture, Bournemouth International Centre, 2002. A recent addition to the gardens in front of the Bournemouth International Centre is this sculpture to honour Lewis Tregonwell, the 'founder' of Bournemouth; Christopher Crabbe Creek, the first town surveyor and Inspector of Nuisances (yes, he is sitting on a toilet); and three sons of Bournemouth who were awarded the Victoria Cross, Sergeant Frederick Charles Riggs, Corporal Cecil Reginald Noble and Lieutenant Colonel Derek Anthony Seagrim. *(Louise Perrin)*

IMAX Cinema, 2002. The latest development on the seafront is the IMAX cinema complex. It opened in 2002 on the site of the old Pier Approach Baths. It also contains bars, restaurants and children's activity areas. *(Russell-Cotes Art Gallery and Museum Collection/Martin Coyne)*

IMAX Cinema, 2002. The development of the IMAX was very controversial. Most of the criticism concerned the loss of the view from Bath Hill of the seafront and across to the Purbecks. *(Russell-Cotes Art Gallery and Museum Collection/Martin Coyne)*

The view from the Bournemouth International Centre across Pier Approach, 2002. As well as heading for the most modern leisure attractions, people continue to enjoy a traditional carousel ride and the ever-popular open-top bus tours. *(Louise Perrin)*

Acknowledgements

I have spoken to many people in the process of compiling this book, following leads and chasing facts. I would like to thank them all for their time and help, especially to those whose photographs I could not eventually use. Next time perhaps?

I would like to record my grateful thanks to those individuals, photographers, companies and organisations who have permitted me to use photographs from their collections and all photographs are acknowledged accordingly.

Finally I would like to acknowledge my debt once again to John Travis, author, researcher, and seaside historian – from little acorns big oaks grow.

I have endeavoured to check all dates and facts, but I would be pleased to hear from anyone who has noticed major discrepancies in facts or figures. The Heritage Zone of the Bournemouth Library has an excellent collection of books on many aspects of local history but I would recommend three in particular for further reading:

John F. Travis, *The Rise of the Devon Seaside Resorts 1750–1900*, University of Exeter Press, 1993

John K. Walton, *The British seaside. Holidays and resorts in the twentieth century*, Manchester University Press, 2000

David S. Young, *The Story of Bournemouth*, Redwood Press Limited, reprinted 1970

> *The toast is*
> *'Absent Friends'*